Pulling a Dragon's Teeth

2002 Agnes Lynch Starrett Prize

Pitt Poetry Series

Ed Ochester, Editor

Pulling a Dragon's Teeth

Shao Wei

University of Pittsburgh Press

The publication of this book is supported by a grant
from the Pennsylvania Council on the Arts

Published by the University of Pittsburgh Press, Pittsburgh, Pa., 15260

Manufactured in the United States of America

Printed on acid-free paper

10 9 8 7 6 5 4 3 2 1

ISBN 0-8229-5835-X

To my hometown and my grandfather

To Galway Kinnell, who teaches me how to sing in English

Contents

1

my steps come back and forth on a piece of sponge

A Fairy Tale

The six-year-old girl sits on her small stool
reading a fairy tale

"I like that place," she takes a spoonful of sugar
licks it slowly
some sugar-flavor gets spilled on the wood floor

Standing on the stool
She looks out of the window
down
on the street close to the Yangtze River
people—strangers—pass by
the city moves, water flows between mountains
no one notices that there is a girl who is studying them
feeling lonely and sad

How could that be?
She tastes the sugar of the world, shares the beauty of
fairy tales, but it is a world
without her

One day
she will know that all of them, no matter of what kind
are from the same place in a woman's body
that produces orgasm or lonely ecstasy
that all of them are going to the same place
some call heaven some call hell

But she will still be lonely
still love the world, with or without her

First Death

The little girl repeats
I do not want to stay by myself
I do not want to stay by myself
She burns the fairy tales, tears her clothes
I will die, I will die if I stay by myself

She murmurs from morning to night
from night to morning
I do not want to die
I do not want to stay by myself

She is talking to me now
Can you stay with me?
No. I want to be alone.

What do you do, then,
make meals for a hard-working fisherman?
have a baby with a peasant?
What can you do?
Bite your fingernail or masturbate at night?

Oh, no, I am diving into myself searching for words that can make bodies burn

So you do something crazy. I hate you. I hate you like this

I hear a hole in my back resonating
wind blows, my back feels chilly
She is still afraid of death
She still doesn't want to stay by herself

My steps come back and forth on a piece of
sponge, lonely insects are drowning on my back

I do not want to die
I do not want to stay by myself

Ten Combs

When morning comes
neighbors are washing their toilet pots outside the doors

I sit by the gate of my grandfather's house
with my ten wood comb friends
which are of different sizes from small to big

I begin to comb my hair with the smallest comb
I call it Mimi
then the second smallest comb
then the third one, fourth, fifth, till the biggest one Tata
I hear music from my hair, and fleas talking in a comic way,
"Shishi, the forest is growing."

Yes, I want to grow it
as long as the hair of the beautiful opera actress
whose body was found in the lily pond
naked but covered by her hair

Comb comb comb
Grow grow grow
My hairs are pushing each other
fleas are stepping on each other
war seems to happen

now, my hair is long enough
I braid it into a long rope
wind it around my waist

At night
I sit by the door
watching the dark street and small yellow lights

hoping someone will come and lead me
to somewhere by the long rope on my back

No one comes
I open my braid
begin to comb my hair, using Tata first
then the second biggest then the third fourth fifth
until the smallest one Mimi

Rice Container

I step onto a chair to lift its heavy cover
but it drops from my hands
kung . . . kung . . .

I cry for the cover of the rice container—
grandfather's old friend
twice a year, he feeds it with a huge bag of rice
telling me, *See, we have enough to eat*

I stand on a higher chair
cling to the edge of the container
and cross, one leg outside, the other inside
one two three, let go
I drop myself into the container and hide there

white rice, and its soft small hands coming into my nose
white rice, and its fat insects tickling my face
white rice, with smell of my grandfather's hand, mother's hand,
and the smell of mold

I bury myself in the rice, looking at the huge hole
a white soft coffin, so comfortable to be in
more rice, more fat insects

I fall asleep in rice as a growing fetus
in an old mother's womb

what will happen to this world
without this girl, this terrible girl, troublemaker
it is even worse without her

my mom is shouting my name on the streets,
among those wild children,
do you see my daughter? do you see our wild duck?

I wake up in rice, like a dead person waking up
before the funeral, stand up to announce:

I am still alive, I want to come back

Rock Holes

the five-year-old girl washes her hands
on the bank of the oldest Xiang Xue Stream—

a variety of rocks sit on the bank
rocks in the shapes of animals, boats, houses
or a violin on a lady's shoulder
each rock has holes
some full of water, some of
sand, some are empty

playing with water in the river,
the little girl listens to a fisherman singing:

"many years ago,
an army of white horses ta ta ta came out of the rock holes
the city was shocked to see them back, wow wow wow
they were missing in a battle a hundred years ago."

the little girl looks at the fisherman's white beard,
how does he know?
is he one of the horses?

"what a journey the white horses have had through the rocks!
what a battle with its soldiers still alive!"

the sun is going home
the riverbank is empty, except the running water and
the girl who is jumping among the rocks
repeating the fisherman's song:

"my home is in a huge stone
every hole opens as a road"

A One-Yuan Fairy-Tale Book

A mermaid with her tail
tossing on the cover of a fairy tale looks at me
on the winter sidewalk

I want to buy this book with my fifty fens
But the old man insists one yuan

He says to himself, stroking his long white beard,
hi, guy, it's not a cheap book,
why should I sell it before I die?

"Please . . ." I beg him, looking back
as if the mermaid will swim away the next minute

We stand face to face, staring at each other
not sure who has to leave first, with or
without this mermaid

Tao Hua and Rooster

my idea of planting a peach tree
comes from the ancient poetry I recite,
Tao Hua, peach blossom, beautiful women

the neighbor's rooster stands by the stone mill
pecking something on the ground
yi? it's my peach pit I planted days ago

I shout at the rooster,
getting a broom in my hand first,
the rooster turns back, ready to fight against me

I curse and wave the broom in the air
the rooster yells at me, kikiki, kikiki
with his widely opened mouth, and red eyes, and waving tail

before my broom reaches him,
his owner, the fat old woman screams in my ear
"what are you doing here, you crazy girl
didn't your grandfather tell you to behave yourself?
it's not your time, not your place"

my peach pit, my peach pit . . .
"fuck you, what's your peach-pit got to do with my dear rooster?
if I find out that he loses a single feather,
your antirevolutionary family will be in trouble . . ."

gegege, wowowo,
the rooster walks to her and is carried away in her fat chest

I hold my wounded peach pit in my hands
waiting for the spring, for the peach
blossom, for Tao Hua blooming

Rotten Apple

At the age of eight,
I had my first apple by the Yangtze River
It was a very big and red fruit
And cheap, only ten fens, half of its body
was gone

The store clerk used his fingers digging into the apple
squeezed its rotten stuff out
Flies ran around as if looking at a miserable bride

I held this apple wandering streets
reluctant to go home, to cut it into pieces, and to share it with someone
It was my first apple, how dear to smell it
as one whole thing for myself

Licking its edge first, a little bit sour, a little bit like medicine
I took one big mouthful from its healthy part
floury, sweet, it reminded me of peasants in the countryside
having a meal by the shit pond, hungry, happy
thankful with rice in their mouths

The apple meat stayed in my mouth for a while
then rushed into my throat
did not desire long intimate battles with my teeth

I started to eat the wound part
sweet and weird
It made me suck harder, then suck and swallow without thinking
What a rotten apple
it made me half joyful, half unsatisfied

Cutting Pumpkins

it's not Halloween
it's a pure game for this child

cut a cross, then another cross
a pumpkin becomes four pieces
take one of them in front of her
cut a cross, another cross
till nobody recognizes a pumpkin

this is not Halloween
not a pure game
this girl learns how to kill
to divide things into smaller things
till nothing is a thing

one day, she grows into a woman
she cuts her talent into pieces
she cuts her melancholy into pieces
she cuts her passion into pieces
until she dies as one thing

2

my finger and i try to criticize each other

English + Chinese

I count the words like a widow's dowry
Poor guy, poor English
even my lovers are more than your words

Wash my heart in the romantic encounter,
skin my body, take off my two angel's wings
let's start from the very beginning

Ask the two to have sex, and see how
the bones particles and organs mix
in language liquid
in which ancient beauties washed their teary faces and men conquered the world
and how I was created

I will borrow
my original voice from Chinese
then begin to learn your sounds, your spellings, with short or long legs
I want to put us together then stir-fry steam and cook for a long time
until everything transforms and redoes both of us

Then it's you who will write the stories or poems
I watch, as a Chinese mermaid
and walk with four feet, two in English, two in Chinese
then we swim in the Sahara Desert we dance on the top of the pyramids

Or simply let's go back to East Sichuan by the Yangtze River
to visit my mom, your mom too
Tell her we are twins we are lovers we are enemies
At best, we are husband and wife
who can torture each other, legally

A Small Finger

My small finger likes to stay in my nose
searching for something
Inside, there might be some minerals the world has awarded me
of which I have not been informed

My finger turns around, like a swimming angel
I feel pleasant
I feel the power of a small finger

One day, I stay with a guy
who likes to talk about postmodern art
As usual, my finger is comfortable in my nose
while he is excited talking
Suddenly he stops and stares at me
My finger is scared as if
it were attacking a wrong place in someone else's body

From then on, my finger and I have a hard time
we try to criticize each other—

"Why do you want to enter my nose?"
"I want to feel inside of you."
"Why do you have a finger like me?"
"I was born with hands with you."

We couldn't find the answer
My small finger still wants to go inside my nose,
still wants to be close to the body it is a part of
There is a little dirt in its small nail,
dirty things from my body or from the world
But is it possible that it might be a life being condensed
like my own life being condensed somewhere else?

The Life Trip of a Plastic Heart

A plastic heart is having its world journey

It gets on a showboat in the Caribbean
The water shines under the red sun
The plastic heart sees a reflection in the water:
"Who is that guy, so great without a heart?"

The plastic heart stands in a corner of the deck
listening to the captain reading Whitman's poems
The heart pities Whitman who slept under his own roof
for the first time at the age of sixty-seven
But today, the world is changing
a plastic heart is better than a human's

The plastic heart boards a bus
Suddenly its former owner is passing by on the street
The heart jumps from the window and tries to chase her
A passing car hits it and it explodes
a red broken plastic bag in the middle of the street

The nearest cinema is playing the Russian movie *Doctor Zhivago*—
When the exiled poet sees Lara on the street,
he jumps out of the bus and chases her
Suddenly he has a heart attack and falls down on the ground
He holds tightly the silent back of his lover in the last moment . . .

So, another plastic heart is ready to start

Farm Chicken

After saying goodbye to this world
I will go to a farm. At its wooden gate,
I will register as a new citizen.

I will get up early to sing.
I only have one word, "kookoo,"
which makes my singing cliché.

In the afternoon
I learn to lay eggs
as big as fists.
But eggs I lay will lack something essential
for them to turn into chickens
for eaters to have a next life.

My eggs will become mice, cats, pigs, or dogs
They will live love work marry.
My children, my chicken children will not suffer what I do.

A king wants to eat a chicken after hunting.
He will walk into the farm.
Every chicken will be talking to him,
wanting to go with him
except me. "What a silent chicken!
She must be wise in heart."

I know it will be the end of my chicken life.
I won't mind serving as a dish to a great king
I clean myself
as if going to see my lover.

The king's cook is a tough man.
He won't kill me with a knife

but force some wine into my mouth,
then pull my feathers easily.
How painful
I can say nothing but "kookoo."

I will choke and faint
and die gradually without
a drop of blood missing.
Such a man
he knows everything
about killing.

I am on a plate now,
delicious and sweet.
My blood preserves my essence
as a chicken and a human once.

Fish Above

The fish lies on a piece of silk
After someone has embroidered it there
it stays like it is at home

When the girl looks at it, its eyes turn around with hers
The four eyes are looking for each other
not afraid at all

The girl's hands touch the silk and
the hands of the person embroidering—
the fish extends its body between her fingers
swimming among the threads, line across line
how silk is woven, how the fish gets a complete body
and its tail in golden yellow

The girl steps back from touching the sunshine
The strong heat begins to burn the fish
the fish burns, burns an hour
The girl's hands are empty
the fish must have swam or flown away,
or turned its body into the girl's

Potato

it is a shy potato
with thin clothes, as yellow as me
potatoes grow everywhere
my potato is different

i wash it in spring water
smell it, and feel its desires under the small skin
it is a potato that can't be made into
cakes or French fries
but can be transformed into energy for lovers
no matter how old they are

i remember the sweat on farmers' backs
they work as hard as they love
my grandfather says planting a potato is planting a life

from then on
i become considerate because of my potato
its small life survives many gigantic lives
and will survive me

my potato keeps its color, size until one day
it grows again in my room
grows white hairs from inside like mine
i can hear my potato calling my nickname
sweet as a singer in a white hall
audiences are my lost ancestors

Square Cauldron

Around midnight, at the opening ceremony
for China's five-thousandth-year exhibition,
I stand before a square cauldron
brown and a little blue
sitting on its throne in a large glass case.

Its body decorated with animals, masks,
and nipples transports me home.
My ancestors cooked in such a pot:
meat and vegetables, stones, red mud,
wild herbs, women's milk, and enemy's bones,
nurturing our bodies and our legends.

Enemies' masks and bones are hung on bamboo sticks.
While water boiled, their women were dancing around the cauldron,
naked, more beautiful than our mothers and grandmothers.
Suddenly, in one corner of the stone hall
a skinned animal is carried in
and thrown into the cauldron:
it screams in the scalding waves.

I step back and bend down
holding my arms closely to my chest
Will I be the next one dropped into the cauldron
or must I jump into it by myself
so I can swim to the other edge of time?

Manhattan, a Small Matchbox

Manhattan is a small matchbox
I put it in my pocket
When I wash clothes in the East River
the small matchbox falls into the water and I can't get it back
So I go to Central Park to look for another one

Central Park is the tomb of an emperor
where I can return to history and look for treasures
I dig mud with my fingers
the emperor is awakened by my noise
Sir, could you help me?
He says nothing but gives me his magic bowl
Inside, Manhattan lies like a red bean

After I get back Manhattan
it is surrounded by walls
walls can walk, can flow like water
Buildings push each other and move like insects
which tickle Manhattan
Manhattan laughs day and night, can't stop

I change it into a reservation
I put three buffaloes near the World Trade Center, two
red birds in Washington Square, a peacock and a panda in mating season

Then I sit down in the six o'clock sunset
enjoying my great project
Suddenly, a silver light stops before me
an Indian man flirting on a white horse
He floats me a red handkerchief that exactly covers my face
I grasp it away and see the man riding toward the low sun
All my animals following him into the sky
I enlarge and enlarge my eyes until my eyeballs
become a part of the sky too

Thinking behind Thinking

Traveling is a traveler's destination

The walls on both sides don't show their faces
I hear a head is being cut down on the tower of a church
survivalists are smiling
the whistling of an unnamed bird sounds closer in the tunnel

On the eighth floor of the Bobst library
I once sat as a newcomer
Facing the huge gray building, the trees below reminded me of my baby sister
whose small watery mouth always bit my shoulder

The clouds must move fast now
the sun's mirror makes us resemble each other
Summer's memory always mingles with sex on grassland or sweaty underwear
Gray, gray, the color of death
suddenly blossoms in early spring

A dog walker carries his half hamburger in a paper
honest people hide behind an arch
coughing the whole night
My trip is half circled toward a village
while I am looking for the first car of the train
looking for the original dream

Pain

Falling down and breaking my foot
I stood up in sweat and walked to the subway
My face was in darkness in the long tunnel
Suddenly I heard a familiar Russian song, "Kaqiusha"
A man was playing his accordion
by his foot, there was a map of the former Russia

My heart sank and sank
until it hit the bottom of my home river Yangtze
I left and I returned
through its spring rapids

I came out of the subway
my heart became soft and hard
like a man's penis in a lover's hand
No Russian man, no Kaqiusha, no home
my foot refused any thinking

One day, I told myself, if I don't want a human's body anymore
I will divide my heart into two parts down the middle
my body into two halves

    But I know
    that day, my pain will be doubled, too

Punctuation

:(colon)

a hurricane on the pillow
a lock of hair, sharp as needles
—(dash)
a heart above a stove, being heated
—(dash)
a dream never dies

love on the paper fan, no blood, no orgasm
a drawing, black and white,
as cold as distance
. . . (ellipsis)
it grows
poisoned mouths, crippled legs,
fallen walls, fishes on the moon
all are guests in this life
this life—not the next one

in the center of the brain,
someone is sucking the juice
playing with the dead dolls

a broken jade ring, a thin china cup
once planted in the garden, rotten in a poem

oh, come on
please let me have a break
, (comma)

what I have
a breath

what I want
a breath
. (period)
, (comma)
. (period)
, (comma)
. . . ellipsis

Wrong Dance

faces   legs   broken hearts
the upturned stage
"Where are you from?"
"From underground"
"Where are you going to?"
"Go to hell," hell hell hell

jazz   cha-cha-cha, sad jazz
sad cha-cha-cha sad dazzling jazz cha-cha-cha

split legs copied faces broken hearts in the village
never knowing who is who
the two are smoking marijuana
a song is humming: "If you know who I am, just follow.
If you don't know who I am,
I am a guest in your bed."

the island is moving under the water
the danger is coming to the journey
dear baby, don't cry, just love me, just do do do
(the old lover stands by the door wearing his black gloves
you know who I am who I am going to be)
be be be

Niagara Falls in Winter

the wild water
like an aged woman desiring a lover she never gets
when she dies
her body freezes like organized bones
but her unfinished shouting   still under the solid skeleton

A Face on the Cafe Window

it's winter, the coldest evening

I see a face floating in the cafe among men and women
waves of human heat beat its wings

the face is lonely in the center, a small and naked face
it reminds me of a woman
who often walked in the village midnights

her companions were always different, one day
a robber tried to rape her and he killed her instead
her two black eyes, thin lips, and an ear on one side
stayed in the village

flyers are everywhere
looking for this woman, or that woman
missing children, vanished wives
a world where misplacement is replacement

a murder seems new, always new to me
as if the knife is in me
people walk, day and night
not noticing that someone is missing

Spirit of Butterflies in Two Parts

1.

it's not the music
I care about, I want to know why they fly

the ancient classmates are only boys
but there is an exception
when one tells the other "he" is "she"
he almost drops his teeth

the story is cut short by people in literature
but it's put into music
on tapes and on stage

it's not the music
I care about, I want to know how they fly

you see the butterflies fly freely
fly deep into summer
when the thunderstorms splash the tomb of
a desperate lover
the girl runs into his tomb
and the two become butterflies and fly
into the bones of their descendants

it's not the music
I care about, I care about how they become butterflies

2.

you fly, on the top of a mountain
you suck the honey of young flowers

you surround me like a flying snake
deep in my back, every pore there

every layer of my skin is burning, peeled by a finger
as thin as a needle
you dress me in layers of clothes
clothes of grief
grief of loss
loss of love
love of madness in music
next door to my poetry

3

how could you leave without saying goodbye

Reciting the Tang Dynasty Poetry

Sitting by the cracked table
I leaned on my grandfather's standing clock

I didn't know what "nostalgia" was
I couldn't feel "the cold moon," or being abandoned
I didn't miss a homeland at war
But I recited the poetry after all

Line by line
I stepped into the river
where nobody replaces anybody
where pebbles, sand, and human beings
come to me in the poetry

Water becomes old
I am at the age of 100
I still think about what "nostalgia" was
I still can't feel "the cold moon," or being abandoned
I still don't miss a homeland at war
But I recite the poetry after all

And I do a little bit more
I put my poetry in the river
I put myself as a tiny fish into the water
swimming swaying my body and singing
How I love to open my fish mouth and recite a poem
from Tang Dynasty
Ah ah ah . . . ah ah ah ah
Ah ah ah ah . . . ah ah ah

Yes, I know what "nostalgia" is
Yes, I feel the cold moon, and being abandoned
Yes, I miss a homeland at war
I recite the poetry after all

Mr. Shao Kang Ning

I called you Gong Gong in Chinese
I called Gong Gong when I learned to speak

Mother's father instead of my father
you gave me your name, Shao
S H A O, from your father, father's father, and further

Xinglong Jie, the Prosperous Road by the Yangtze River
had long winters, always was foggy in the morning
I woke up and saw Gong Gong cooking and washing before going to work

Shao Kang Ning, my Gong Gong, a country boy
came to the city as an apprentice. Years later
you bought a house for your parents
and became the first capitalist on Xinglong Jie,
which was renamed Anti-Revisionism Road after 1949

Gong Gong became the target of revolution,
Your printing factory, rubber, paper, ink, and Chinese characters
all belonged to the nation now
What a shame to be rich while the majority was poor
Gong Gong was liberated in the 1980s
and was given back everything. Xinglong Jie came back too

A faithful follower of Confucius,
"education is the highest among a million activities"
You wanted us children to study hard, read useful books,
and divided your salary as our study allowance

I was the first in our family to go abroad
and study in New York

You dreamed of the American president
telling him to take care of your proud kid

On September 22 1997, I called home as usual
I was told "Gong Gong *si le* on September 16, and was buried in the mountain today"

September 16 was the Chinese Mid-Autumn Festival
for family reunions
Xinglong Jie knelt down in front of the grave of Shao Kang Ning
everyone cried for you, the oldest man who valued paper, books, and
education

Except me

I was sick in New York, dreaming of a small ghost
with ten hands and ten feet
smiling singing and dancing around me

Is that you, Gong Gong?

Innocent Mother

She walks through Dianbao Road into the brick building
under the neighbors' eyes
She is twenty-five years old, coming back to her parents' home with a baby
her husband is in prison

Her hair is in braids mixed with lucky red threads
like a tailed cloud in the gray street of 1965
Her mother, very sick, watches the second daughter silently
and takes over her baby

She starts to work hard in an iron factory with a group of men
They tease her, her shyness and her misfortune
Her face becomes as cold as a piece of iron, her life
withers when she is still young and
beautiful, but heavy enough to sink
in the quiet hometown

Midnights, she comes home through empty streets
the dim streetlights shine on her face
then on the face of her three-month-old baby
who cries the whole night, sobbing and waiting for someone to
hold her, the grandmother is so tired
and falls asleep in an old bamboo chair while the baby
sucks her fingers

She is tired too. She goes to the kitchen quietly
for some leftover rice, cold and not enough
Then she slides into her bed by the window
In a bed next to hers, her father is snoring

She sees a star very close to her
She sleeps very well, a woman with dreams again

She is not told that her mother will pass away in three days
That night, my twenty-five-year-old mother doesn't think of her future
she takes a deep breath. So deep, as if for her whole life

"Fascist" Aunt

my twenty-eight-year-old aunt is beautiful but can't find a husband
she dates a lot of guys, rich, smart, or handsome
but with nonrevolutionary family blood

this summer, she dates a good guy, son of a poor peasant
when they meet for the first time
he blushes and lowers his head, almost dropping his glasses

Can you carry her? my aunt points at me
"She goes with us?"
Yes, my sister still works

we come to the chilly riverbank
the guy unfolds his handkerchief on one stone stair
"You sit here." *How about her?*
he looks around and replies shyly
"Can she sit on my knees?"

proud aunt sits on the guy's handkerchief, talking
while folding a mouse with her own handkerchief
—my toy as a small kid
it jumps cutely in her hand

woops, the mouse drops on the ground, falling down a few stairs
the guy runs to catch it, again and again
after a while, he is sweating, his glasses foggy
and his face shining under the sun

naughty aunt has an idea. She points at the second button of her shirt
Can you tell what color this button is?

the guy opens his eyes widely. could not tell
he takes away his glasses and bends his upper body

toward my aunt who moves backward little by little
the guy bends forward and forward until both
of them lose balance and roll down the stairs

aunt, are you ok?
my aunt laughs and coughs down there
You, you blind guy, blind, how can I marry a guy like you?
Over, everything is over. OK, let's go home.

it's dusk in the small city,
ships in the Yangtze are whistling leaving messages
people wave goodbye to their beloved ones
we travel back through narrow up-and-down streets by the river
my aunt walks first, with a broken toe
the guy second with his oily face
I sleep on his back, too young to understand a life

I Wear My Mother's New Coat

We get Mom's new coat from the tailor
Mom lets me wear it first
We put it on me, it touches my feet

I wish the coat could be smaller
so it fits me better
Mom wishes it could be bigger
so she could wear it winter after winter

The dark blue coat walks with me
I feel like the princess of the small town
I'm the only child of my mom
the child who reads big books and grows a dream

Imagine this is a magic coat—
there come piles of new books
and colorful birds with good luck for Mom and me . . .

Suddenly I see two classmates on the street
who yelled "prisoner's daughter" at me in school
I try to shrink in the coat as small as a black pea

Magically the two girls don't see me and walk away
I look at Mom who knows nothing
She stops me and bends down
picking a white thread from the coat

I stare at her, her face, thin and pale
Her hands, swollen with chilblains,
touch the coat and the new buttons gently
instead of hugging me

I become mad and begin to scream
she cares for her coat more than me
I kick and tear the coat hysterically
"What are you doing?"
She yells and I yell too
not wanting to give the coat back to her

until
today

The Father

1.

gossipy neighbors stand in front of our door
talking to me,
Hi, your father is coming back
ho ho ho

father?
I am more familiar with ghosts
ghosts in stories than a father

I pull out my doll box from under my small bed
if my dolls don't have a father, why should I?

does mom know this?
is she afraid?

the moon is always big when I feel lonely
I measure the distance between us
everyone is busy earning a living
no time to care about a girl and her dreams

even ghosts have dreams
even ghosts need colors
even ghosts want to fly

why shouldn't I?

but I don't need a father

2.

He came back from jail after eight years
when my morning was quiet
when my childhood was complete without a father

"Call me Father"
"Call me"
"Call"
I refused and he slapped my face

We went to his mother's funeral in the old town
How could he look at me in that way—
as if I were a woman,

That night is the only night
the daughter and the father stayed together in one room
I couldn't sleep
worrying a ready hand might touch me in the darkness

"If you continue to follow me, I'll throw you into the Yangtze."
I remember the fire of anger in his eyes
He was supposed to give me the monthly allowance
But he ran away for a meeting with some woman

I dared not go home with empty hands,
and bent down on the stone stairs by the harbor
my tears followed the flowing water
as if looking for a witness

I was not a safe child anymore
If he wanted to take back my life
I promised
I would return it to him
as a gift

The Absent Goodbye

How could you leave without saying goodbye

I run through the streets
in Wanxian City, through the old houses on Dianbao Road
as if playing a childhood game among the empty coffins on the dusty top floor
until I find all your windows are sealed

The snow is falling slowly
The sunshine jumps on the roof of our old house
You're starting the fire to cook a potato for me
after I am back from school

Dear old man, once you are my grandfather
you are my grandfather forever
I don't care how much older you are than me

When we were both younger
I hated you for being so strict
It was hard
Nobody taught us how to love the beloved ones

I heard you snoring in your huge wooden bed
I counted one by one hoping that
you would stop and I could sleep peacefully

Many winter nights, you and I, the only man and the little woman
I wanted to go to your bed
to warm my feet
I knew you needed warmth too
But you didn't say, come

I left home for a long journey
looking for a warm bed like yours

I slept in different beds
bigger than yours or smaller than yours
with people
whom I loved or did not love

But nobody snored like you
Nobody was as strict as you
concerning what kind of person I should grow into
And, eventually, nobody was like you, leaving
in sleep without saying goodbye

Dear Death,

Do you remember those nights, our first encounters
a little girl in her grandfather's big dark room, reading with a flashlight
or by the streetlamps through the window,
refusing to go to bed
You come,
saying, *if you sleep, I will take you away*

Instead, you take people away from me
one, two, and three, while I'm struggling with you

Just like yesterday: my ninety-three-year-old grandfather is still
snoring loudly in his wooden bed
He likes to cut his goatee with a pair of old scissors
smiling like a student, "I'm working now."
He looks at me from over his brown plastic glasses
which I clean with my sniffly sleeves

Sun Gong Gong and his wife babysat me for years
He dies in my hometown—mine, not his—
his wife after one month dies too
On the stone arch bridge I walk toward his home,
feeling him holding my hand and showing me around
Him, a sixty-five-year-old man without his own child
Me, a three-year-old girl without a father

Last night,
I dreamt of them all
walking behind a glass wall, without eyes and ears
I cried on the other side, calling them
come back or let me go with you

Dear death, after all these years,
your power still surrounds me like a uniformed army

I'm still that girl, reading, having a hard time getting to sleep
If you take them away from me,
why don't you take us all?

Dear death, thanks for your valuable attention

Sincerely yours

4

brother, can i call you brother

Making Love

he raised his head from sweat
leaving me in water
bottomless and painfully dark

the flowing river now
is quiet like a faceless infant
"I love you," "love" is an echo in the room

the tired starlight on his bare shoulders
reminds me of a day   of a place in an old story
a battle of bodies
an endless war

Horse Riding

You are too humble to come
even grass came, even bees and sand
but never you

I hold your neck tightly
wet and warm, too juicy and mature
We are like two lovers, just out of work

You move one step, I move one step
We are supposed to move
together, either backward or forward

The moon's face is round, the moon's face is
half round
We run along the coastline
deep into the heart of another land

Brother, can I call you brother
You choose the direction, I follow
As soon as I hear your
whinnying
your piercing sound breaks me into pieces
Each of me will ride on your back
until the road ends

Sunflower Bitch

when storms are boiling in the sky
when cooked seeds grow into trees
all stars exile in an unknown space

sunflower bitch
you eat flesh of baby bulls, seeds of unripe fruits, standing by the edge of the earth
shouting, I AM SUNFLOWER BITCH WHAT CAN YOU DO TO ME

your eyes are as white as flesh
as dark as bone
being chased by killers like water, fire, lovers, and disgust
your continuous dreams are about stone, assassinating, and the birth of waves

you touch the water with your toes, shocked as if on fire, WOW, SUCH A BITCH

way of living, way of exiling
haha, what can you say, you sunflower bitch
your lovers are hanged in your backyard
you collect their eyeballs to make buttons on your nightgown
the tongues of birds, the hands of small ants
are cooked over and over on the stove

brother, mother, sister, and lover
you curse everyone you make wrong spellings
you bitch you
you kill the sunshine, you smash it in your palm
go, you say, you blow bad fortunes toward hardworking people
mother is dying, father is dying, you sunflower bitch is dying who else is dying

HELP HELP

sunflower bitch
you see how deep how dark how marvelous and amazing

if you call your name again and again
do you see horses run emotionally, widows commit suicide
do you see the sleeping sheep stay in the empty mountain
and fog-eating shadows around them
are you afraid, are you?

look, the sun the moon the man and woman are being thrown to you
you'd better open your door to accept all of them
the door the widely opened door will make you big
as big as the earth as big as the time
as big as you, sunflower bitch

now, look at your mouth, your hundreds of teeth are broken
your smiles toward the sun make the earth shake
make all deaths flee, all hearts become wild
you bitch you sunflower last bitch
hate you no more than this

A Way to Love

It is my turn to be quiet
When you enter me slowly
I feel my land being plowed so deep
so accurately
I breathe with my nose, not with my tightly closed mouth
You hold your breath cruelly
your whole body is on one point of me,
like a robot on the stage
My legs rise up higher and higher
like a soldier waving her flag happily

No matter what happens, I would hold you firmly in me
"No way to get out," you said, "no way"
Then stay, stay until the trees open
until the fruits burgeon

Chasing in the Wind

The cloud looks like an angry girl
who is pulling her hair and tearing her blue dress
Her witch's eyes are enlarged like stars

She fires at me. She throws
sand, sound, rotten leaves on my shaky body
Her broken skirt covers the Hudson River
by which I sit down to cure my homesickness

My God, an old man behind me cries, running
with his eyes shut
His hat is flying away from his head
I start to run too,
chasing wind in the wind, like chasing water in the water

Like water chasing boats in the river
or boats chasing water
like I chase myself in the wind
in such a day

It was my dream as a little girl by the Yangtze River
to be a woman who would stay where she was born
whose chimney would always be smoking
whose shoes would be too tight for her to walk out of her home
whose grandfather would never die
without saying goodbye

Mountain after mountain
river after river
I've walked too far,
my face ripe in the wind, in the chasing
I am ripe in the wind, in the chasing . . .

The sky is blue now
The wild girl is gone
and my shoes fill with sand
So I walk heavily
like just waking up from a long night's sex

Where is the love
where is the home, where is the father, brother
supporter and sister
Like an adopted child
I always feel the absence

Open my arms, open my chest
I hold the wind, I become pregnant
ready to chase and to be chased again

Mountain, River, and Unfinished Flowers

1.

Wind blows heavily from northwest of the river
Big Brother and his wife are drinking water

A skinny girl stands knocking
by the door, red as radish, her hands are shaking

"Come in, girl, have a cup of green tea."
"Come in, girl, continue your journey tomorrow."

The pretty girl sleeps overnight in the house
The three have a wonderful dream

When the sun shines the next morning
the couple chats about where to build their cemetery

"The land with the river view should be good."
"But not as good as by the mountain."

Looking over the river or leaning by the mountain
both are good but not good enough

A strong smell is dancing in the air
as if spring returns

Big Brother searches
and finds the girl is gone

In the room where she stayed
there are flowers growing

Yellow flowers, pink flowers, flowers with tiny buds
skinny branches and without leaves

2.

Spring comes,
Big Brother returns to the mountain for herbs and seeds

He digs everywhere with baby green leaves
drinks every drop of twinkling dew

One hole in the ground is too deep to see
he pulls the grass hard out of the earth

A strong light shines straight at his head
his gray hair turns black

A soft pearl appears in his hand
a pearl as big as Big Brother's fist

Big Brother hurries home, his mind full of questions
His wife shakes her head, "I've never seen such a thing."

His pearl continues to grow
His flowers never wither

3.

Big Brother turns one hundred years old
his wife one hundred and two

Every morning, the flowers blow wind into the house
Every night, the pearl sings songs, boats stop to listen

People come to buy Big Brother's flowers
to look at his pearl and cure diseases

The Devil is jealous of Big Brother's treasures
The Devil comes to rob the pearl to destroy the flowers

The flowers are crushed under the Devil's feet
They grow with fresher and quieter smiles

Big Brother hides the pearl in his mouth
the pearl falls into his stomach

When Big Brother becomes thirsty, he drinks all the water in the house
He comes to drink by the river, one mouthful another mouthful

Suddenly, a big wave comes and sweeps Big Brother into the river
"Come back, my old man, come back," his wife cries

Big Brother struggles in the water
he turns his head back ninety times

A dragon jumps out of the water where he disappears
The dragon wears a beard like Big Brother's

The mountain mother is crying, the river mother is crying
Big Brother is gone, everything is changed

4.

Flowers bloom and grow huge
Big Brother's wife turns one hundred and twenty

Every day, she sends flowers to the river
until there comes a huge flood

Half of the mountain is in water
The river becomes an ocean of tears

Flowers are scattered everywhere
a floating net for Big Brother's wife to stay

They carry her across tides and currents
They carry her between two high cliffs

After the floods retreat, Big Brother's wife
finds two coffins under an orange tree

A dragon's body stays fresh inside one coffin
In the other one, there is the pearl

Big Brother's wife follows its shining
She lies down and puts the pearl in her mouth

At night, the two coffins are carried together
across two mountains, looking over the river

Big Brother's wife closes her eyes
sees Big Brother on top of the water

They smile to each other
Two mountains come together

Acknowledgments

The author wishes to acknowledge the editors and publishers of the following journals, in which some of these poems previously appeared:

> *Brooklyn Rail* ("Spirit of Butterfly Lovers"); *Die Aussenseite Des Elementes* ("A Way to Love" in English and German); *Greetings* ("Cutting Pumpkins," "First Death," "Fish Above," "The Life Trip of a Plastic Heart," "A One-Yuan Fairy-Tale Book," "Potato," "Rice Container," "Rock Holes," and "Rotten Apple"); *Hanging Loose Press* ("Farm Chicken," "A Small Finger," and "Ten Combs"); *Homestead Review* ("Chasing in the Wind" and "Horse Riding"); *Parnassus* ("Square Cauldron"); *revolution & evolution* ("First Death," "First Life," and "Pain"); *Seneca Review* ("A Way to Love"); *Washington Square* ("Sunflower Bitch").

I feel grateful to the Creative Writing Program at New York University for giving me the opportunity to start my journey in this country and in English; to Jane Cooper and other friends who read this manuscript and offered valuable opinions; and to the Agnes Lynch Starrett Poetry Prize, Mr. Ed Ochester, my editor, and everyone else at the University of Pittsburgh Press.

SHAO WEI was born and grew up in Wanxian City, a small, mountainous city located at the legendary East Sichuan Province by the Yangtze River, half of which is going to disappear with the construction of the new Three Gorges Dam. She came to America in 1996 and got her M.A. in creative writing from New York University. Shao Wei's poems and other writings have been published in China, Hong Kong, Taiwan, and Germany. She has published a limited-edition poetry collection in Chinese, *Nine Songs. Female* (Hong Kong, 1993), and a work of nonfiction, *Culture Bird—Looking for Myself in New York* (Beijing, 2000). She is the recipient of a 1999 Rona Jaffe Foundation Writers' Award, a 2001 New York Foundation for the Arts Fellowship, and a Fredrica Clifton Fellowship at Squaw Valley Community of Writers. She lives in New York, teaching and writing bilingually.